THE SUN

MURRAY "OAK" TAPETA

OUTER SPACE

NORWOOD HOUSE PRESS

Cataloging-in-Publication Data

Names: Tapeta, Murray.
Title: The sun / Murray Tapeta.
Description: Buffalo, NY : Norwood House Press, 2026. | Series: Outer space | Includes glossary and index.
Identifiers: ISBN 9781978574922 (pbk.) | ISBN 9781978574939 (library bound) | ISBN 9781978574946 (ebook)
Subjects: Sun--Juvenile literature.
Classification: LCC QB521.5 T374 2026 | DDC 523.7--dc23

Published in 2026 by
Norwood House Press
2544 Clinton Street
Buffalo, NY 14224

Copyright © 2026 Norwood House Press
Designer: Rhea Magaro
Editor: Kim Thompson

Photo credits: Cover, p. 1 robert_s; p. 5 NASA; p. 6 Ahsious_786/Shutterstock.com; p. 7 Sergey Nivens/Shutterstock.com; pp. 8, 12 Triff/Shutterstock.com; p. 9 buradaki/Shutterstock.com; p. 11 New Africa/Shutterstock.com; p. 13 Digital Images Studio/Shutterstock.com; pp. 14, 15 Evgeny Atamanenko/Shutterstock.com; p. 17 Alones/Shutterstock.com; p. 18 Paopano/Shutterstock.com; pp. 19, 21 muratart/Shutterstock.com;

All rights reserved. No part of this book may be reproduced in any form without permission in writing from the publisher, except by a reviewer.

Printed in the United States of America

Some of the images in this book illustrate individuals who are models. The depictions do not imply actual situations or events.

CPSIA compliance information: Batch #CSNHP26: For further information contact Norwood House Press at 1-800-237-9932.

TABLE OF CONTENTS

Where Is the Sun?..4

How Old Is the Sun? 8

What Is the Sun Like? 12

Has the Sun Been Explored? 18

Glossary 22

Thinking Questions..23

Index...24

About the Author 24

Where Is the Sun?

At the center of our **solar system** is the star Sol. We call it the Sun. More than a million Earths could fit in the space taken up by the Sun!

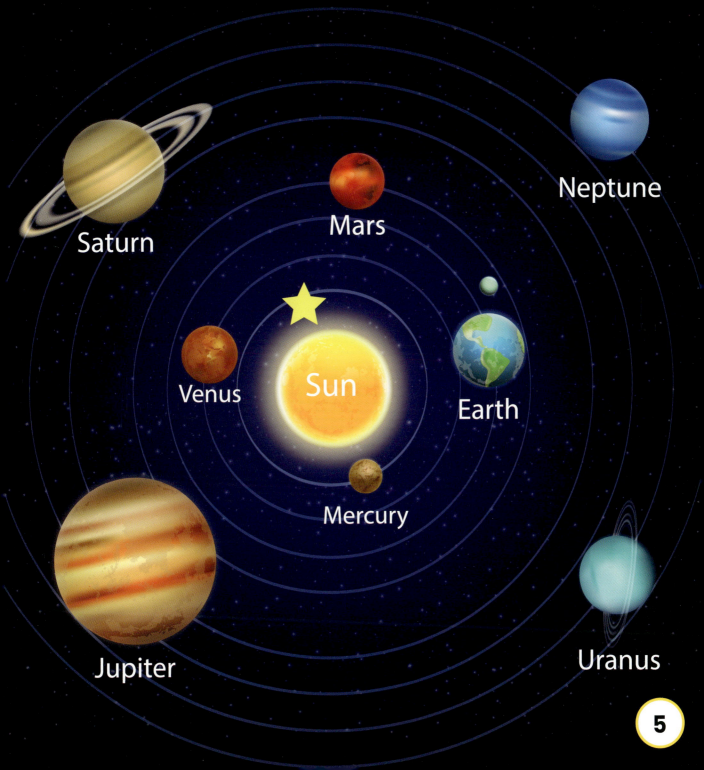

The Sun is about 93 million miles (149 million kilometers) away from Earth. A trip to the Sun from Earth would take several months.

The Sun's **gravity** makes everything in our solar system **orbit** around it. The Sun orbits the center of the Milky Way **galaxy**. Its orbit takes about 230 million Earth years.

How Old Is the Sun?

The Sun is a yellow dwarf star. It formed nearly five billion years ago. It was made from a spinning cloud of gas and dust called a **nebula**.

The nebula broke up. Most of its material got pulled toward the center and became the Sun. The leftovers formed planets, moons, and other objects.

The Sun is in the middle of its life. In about five billion years, it will swell. It will become a different kind of star called a red giant.

What Is the Sun Like?

The Sun is hot! It is hot enough to make any material turn into a gas. Its **core** is about 27 million degrees Fahrenheit (15 million degrees Celsius).

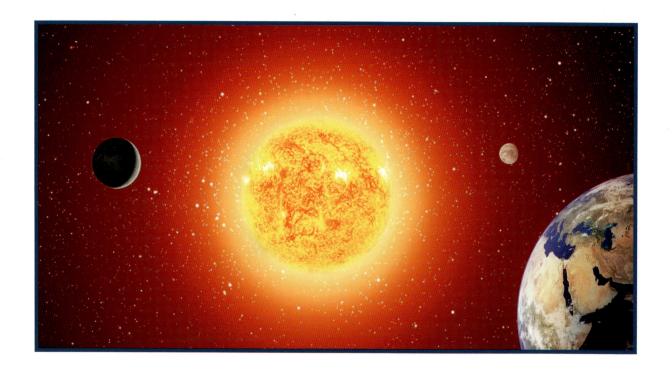

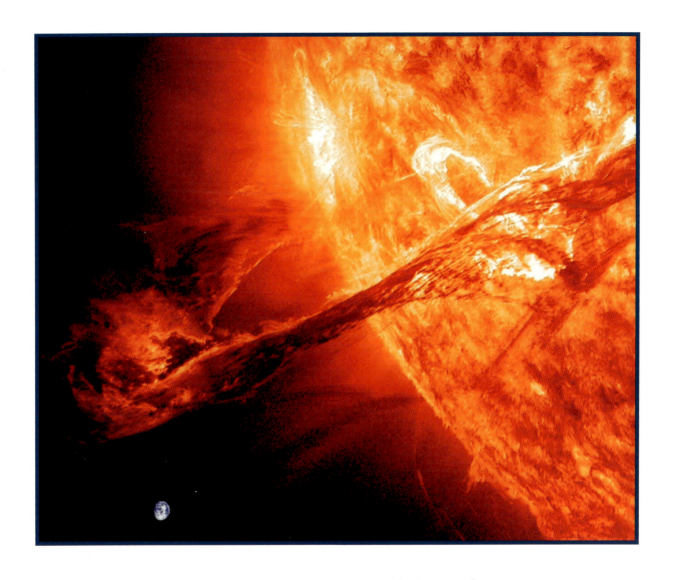

The Sun does not have a solid surface.

It is made of gases.

Explosions in the Sun turn **hydrogen** into **helium**. **Energy** is created in the form of light and heat.

Energy from the Sun takes about eight minutes to reach Earth. It makes life on Earth possible.

At certain times, the Sun is very active. There can be big explosions. These are called solar flares. Black spots can appear on the Sun. These are called sunspots.

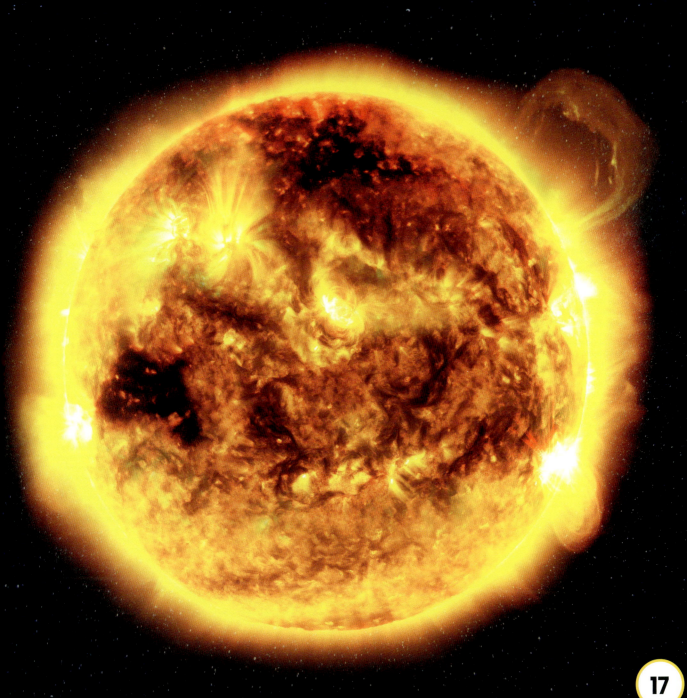

Has the Sun Been Explored?

Nothing can get close to the Sun. It is too hot and bright. **Satellites** study the Sun from a distance. They send data back to Earth.

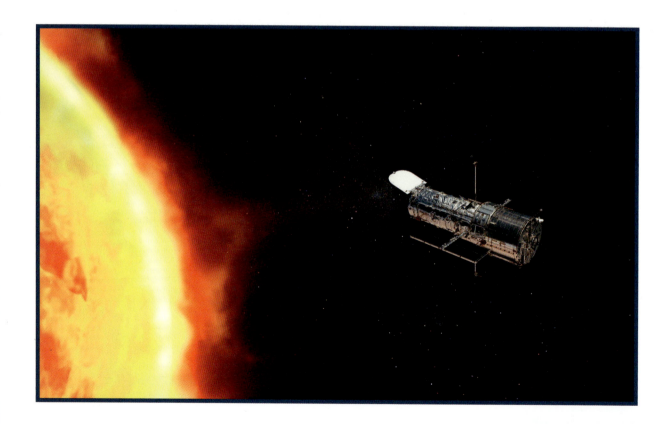

The *SOHO* satellite went to space in 1995. It has studied the Sun ever since. The *Parker Solar Probe* went out in 2018. It has come closer to the Sun than any other **spacecraft**.

Scientists want to keep learning about the Sun. They want to understand the bright star at the center of our solar system.

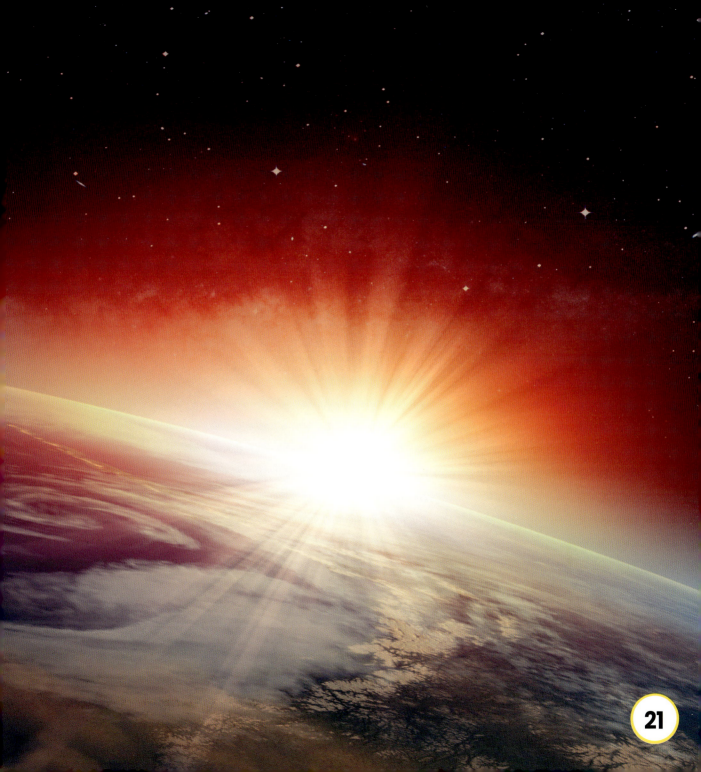

Glossary

core (kor): most inner part; center

energy (EN-ur-jee): power

galaxy (GAL-uhk-see): a very large group of stars and the planets that orbit around those stars

gravity (GRAV-i-tee): an invisible force that pulls objects toward each other and keeps them from floating away

helium (HEE-lee-uhm): a light, colorless gas that does not burn

hydrogen (HYE-druh-juhn): a gas with no smell or color that is lighter than air and that easily catches fire

nebula (NEB-yuh-luh): a cloud of dust and gas in space

orbit (OR-bit): to follow a curved path around a larger body in space

satellites (SAT-uh-lites): spacecrafts sent into orbit around a planet, moon, or other object in space

solar system (SOH-lur SIS-tuhm): the Sun and everything that orbits around it

spacecraft (SPAYS-kraft): a vehicle that travels through space

Thinking Questions

1. What kind of star is the Sun?

2. What keeps Earth and the other planets orbiting the Sun?

3. How was the Sun formed?

4. How does the Sun make energy?

5. Why is the Sun important to Earth?

Index

Earth 4, 6, 15, 18

energy 14, 15

gravity 7

Milky Way 7

Parker Solar Probe 19

SOHO 19

solar flares 16

star 4, 8, 10, 20

sunspots 16

temperature 12, 18

About the Author

Murray "Oak" Tapeta was born in a cabin without plumbing in Montana. Growing up in the great outdoors, he became a lover of nature. He earned the nickname "Oak" after climbing to the top of an oak tree at the age of three. Oak loves to read and write. He has written many books about events in history and other subjects that fascinate him. He prefers spending time in the wilderness with his dog Birchy.